A CONTINENT OF CREATURES

The Animals of
SOUTH
AMERICA

Amie Jane
Leavitt

PURPLE TOAD
PUBLISHING

SOUTH AMERICA

Venezuela
Colombia
Guyana
Suriname
French Guiana
Ecuador
Peru
Brazil
Bolivia
Paraguay
Chile
Argentina
Uruguay
Falkland Islands

North America
Europe
Asia
Atlantic Ocean
Africa
Pacific Ocean
South America
Indian Ocean
Australia
Antarctica

The Amazon is home to the "river monster," the piranha **(per-AH-nuh)** fish. Their teeth are as sharp as sharks' teeth.

Welcome to South America! This continent stretches from just above the equator all the way down to Cape Horn.

South America is made up of dry deserts and rain forests. The Amazon River flows across the land. It is longer than the United States is wide. It is home to millions of kinds of animals.

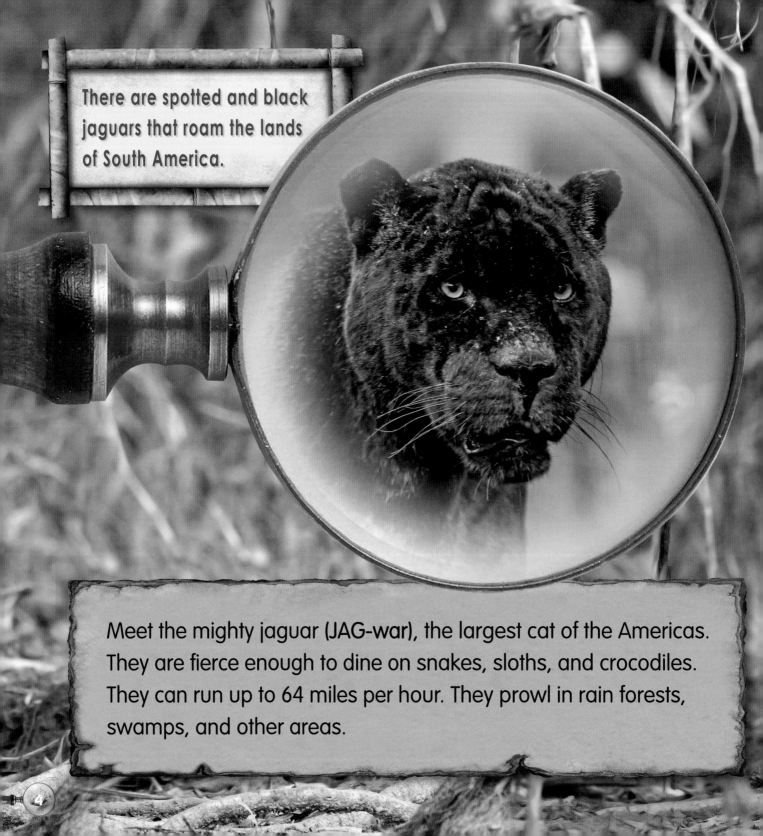

There are spotted and black jaguars that roam the lands of South America.

Meet the mighty jaguar (JAG-war), the largest cat of the Americas. They are fierce enough to dine on snakes, sloths, and crocodiles. They can run up to 64 miles per hour. They prowl in rain forests, swamps, and other areas.

The Atacama (ah-tah-KAH-mah) Desert is in Chile (CHIL-ay). Part of the desert did not have any rain for 400 years! Still, there are lakes here. Flamingos (fla-MING-ohz) live near these lakes. These birds have long, skinny legs and bright pink feathers. They get their pink coloring from the food they eat.

Some flamingos live on nature preserves in the Atacama.

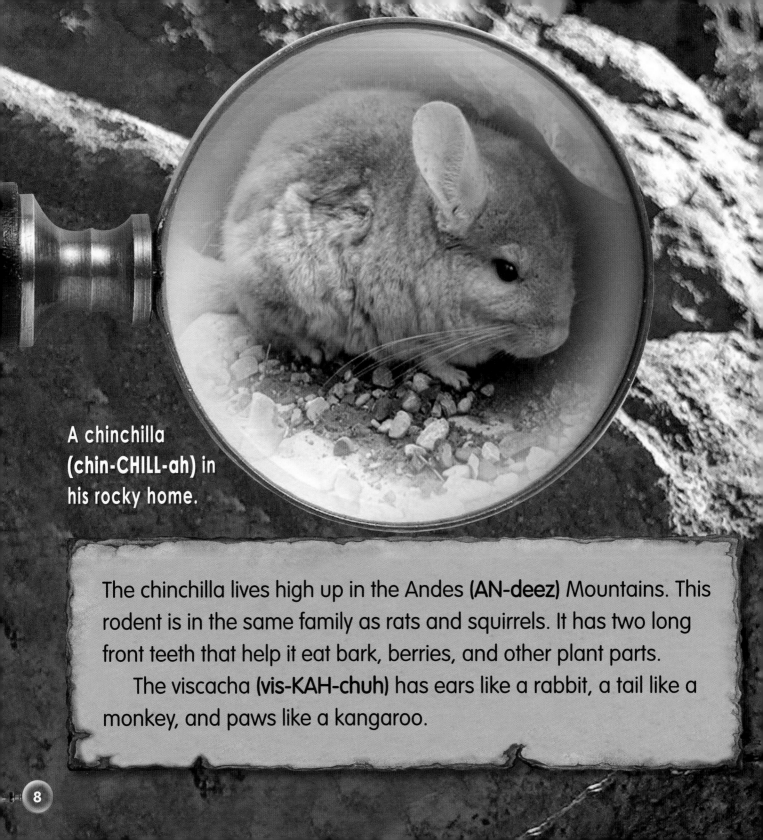

A chinchilla
(chin-CHILL-ah) in
his rocky home.

The chinchilla lives high up in the Andes **(AN-deez)** Mountains. This rodent is in the same family as rats and squirrels. It has two long front teeth that help it eat bark, berries, and other plant parts.

The viscacha **(vis-KAH-chuh)** has ears like a rabbit, a tail like a monkey, and paws like a kangaroo.

Viscachas bounce from rock to rock in their mountain home.

Alpacas (al-PACK-ahz) and llamas (LAH-maz) also live in the Andes. They can live in places with very little water.

Alpacas are smaller than llamas. They weigh only about 150 pounds. Llamas weigh about 400 pounds. Alpacas have very soft fur. Llamas have coarse fur that is used to make rugs and clothing.

Alpacas have very soft fur. Llamas (on left) have coarser fur. Both types are used to make warm clothing.

Condors keep a keen eye on the land below as they look for food.

The Andean condor lives in mountains, deserts, and along the coasts. This scavenger is a type of vulture. It eats all kinds of dead animals.

The condor is one of the largest flying birds. It weighs up to 33 pounds and stretches 10 feet from wing tip to wing tip. It likes to fly in windy areas. The wind helps it stay in the air.

Rockhopper
penguins really
do get around by
hopping.

The southernmost part of South America is Cape Horn. Several types of penguins live near Cape Horn.

The rockhopper penguin (PEN-gwin) lives on Penguin Island. This is one of the smallest penguins in the world. It is only about 20 inches tall when fully grown. Spiky yellow and black feathers grow on top of its head.

The golden dart frog is poisonous.

The imperial tortoise **(im-PEER-ee-uhl TORT-us)** beetle hides its legs and head when its attacked, just like a tortoise.

Near the equator, most of the land is a rain forest. This steamy jungle and its rivers are rich in animal life. Many of these animals are brightly colored: lemon yellow frogs, bright blue beetles, and rainbow-striped fish.

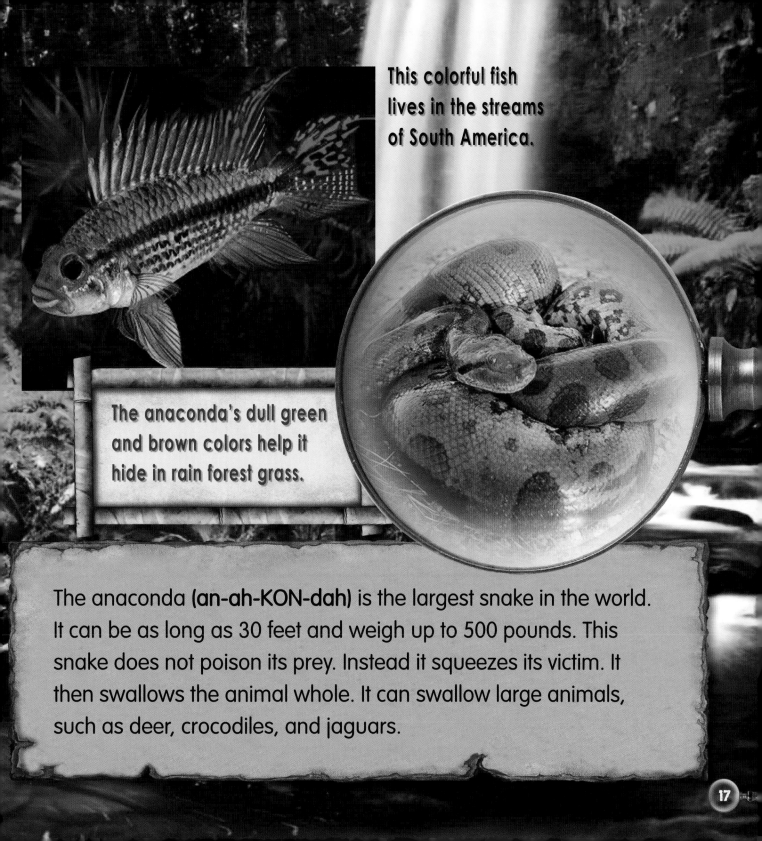

This colorful fish lives in the streams of South America.

The anaconda's dull green and brown colors help it hide in rain forest grass.

The anaconda (an-ah-KON-dah) is the largest snake in the world. It can be as long as 30 feet and weigh up to 500 pounds. This snake does not poison its prey. Instead it squeezes its victim. It then swallows the animal whole. It can swallow large animals, such as deer, crocodiles, and jaguars.

Long arms make sloths good swimmers, too.

Two-toed and three-toed sloths live in the rain forest. Sloths spend most of their life hanging from tree branches. They are the slowest-moving mammals on earth. Sloths sleep up to 20 hours a day!

Sloths stay so still that green algae actually grows on their fur. The color helps them hide from predators.

This sloth has three toes — look at those long nails!

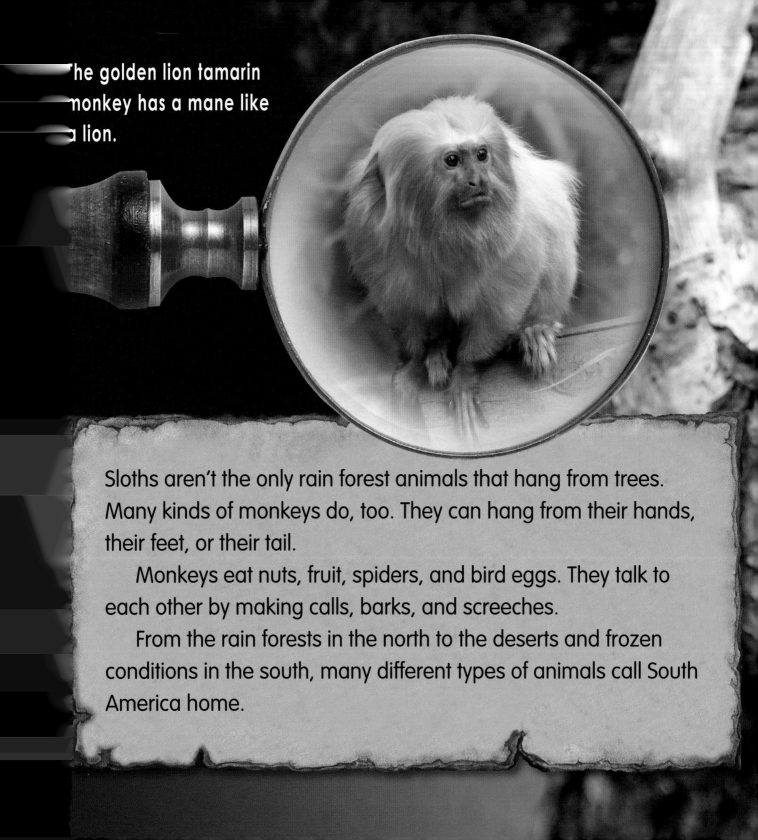

The golden lion tamarin monkey has a mane like a lion.

Sloths aren't the only rain forest animals that hang from trees. Many kinds of monkeys do, too. They can hang from their hands, their feet, or their tail.

Monkeys eat nuts, fruit, spiders, and bird eggs. They talk to each other by making calls, barks, and screeches.

From the rain forests in the north to the deserts and frozen conditions in the south, many different types of animals call South America home.

This cotton-top tamarin
monkey weighs less than
one pound.

FURTHER READING

Books

Aloian, Molly. *A Rainforest Habitat.* Washington, D. C.: National Geographic School Publishers, 2010.

Gibbs, Maddie. *Flamingos, Safari Animals.* New York: Rosen PowerKids Press, 2011.

Gregory, Josh. *Sloths.* New York: Scholastic, 2015.

The Lonely Planet Kids Travel Book: Mind-Blowing Stuff on Every Country in the World. New York: Lonely Planet, 2015.

Perkins, Chloe. *Living in Brazil.* New York: Simon Schuster, 2016.

On the Internet

FactZoo: South American Animals

    http://www.factzoo.com/wild-animal-pictures/south-america

National Geographic: Animals

    http://animals.nationalgeographic.com/

The National Zoo: Amazonia

    https://nationalzoo.si.edu/Animals/Amazonia/

algae (AL-jee)—Simple plants that do not have roots, stems, leaves, or flowers. They generally live in water, in large groups.

biome (BY-ohm)—Regions of the world that have similar climates, animals, and plants.

equator (ee-KWAY-ter)—The middle band of the Earth that is the same distance from both poles.

predator (PREH-deh-ter)— An animal that hunts other animals for food.

scavenger (SKAA-ven-jer)—An animal that eats dead animals.

vulture (VUL-chur)— A large bird of prey that feeds on dead or dying animals.

PHOTO CREDITS: Cover, pp. 1, 4, 16—Tambako the Jaguar; p. 2—Heather Paul ; p. 4—Charles J. Sharp; p. 6—Elrond, Carlos Urzuna; p. 8—Madeleine Deaton; p.10—Matthew Straubmuller; p. 12—Eric Kilby; p. 16—ASM Monteiro; p. 18—Leyo, Christian Mehlfuhrer; p. 20—Marie Hale, Liknes. All other photos—Public Domain. Every measure has been taken to find all copyright holders of material used in this book. In the event any mistakes or omissions have happened within, attempts to correct them will be made in future editions of the book.

INDEX

Printing   1   2   3   4   5   6   7   8   9

The Animals of Africa
The Animals of Antarctica
The Animals of Asia
The Animals of Australia
The Animals of Europe
The Animals of North America
The Animals of South America

ABOUT THE AUTHOR: Amie Jane Leavitt graduated from Brigham Young University and is an accomplished author, researcher, and photographer. She has written more than 60 books for kids, has contributed to online and print media, and has worked as a consultant, writer, and editor for numerous educational publishing and assessment companies. To check out a listing of Amie's current projects and published works, visit her website at www.amiejaneleavitt.com.

Publisher's Cataloging-in-Publication Data
Leavitt, Amie Jane.
   South America / written by Amie Jane Leavitt.
      p. cm.
Includes bibliographic references, glossary, and index.
ISBN 9781624692727
1. Animals—South America—Juvenile literature. I. Series: A continent of creatures.
   QL235 2017
   591.98

eBook ISBN: 9781624692734

Library of Congress Control Number: 2016937187